FIRST FRENCH

chez moi

Consultant: Véronique Leroy-Bennett

LORENZ BOOKS

Contents

Learning French

Introduce your child to French from an early age by combining everyday words and phrases with lively photographs of daily activities in and around the home. Your child will enjoy learning French. Let them look at the pictures and read and remember the French words and phrases that accompany them. Encourage them to say the words aloud.

 A NEW LANGUAGE

In our increasingly global society, the technology of communications evolves so fast that we are in contact with other countries more and more. There is a growing need to understand and speak a second language. For this reason, every child should have an opportunity early in life to have access to a new language. This book will support reading and writing during childhood and school years. Recent research indicates that children are most receptive to linguistic learning between the ages of two and eight. The younger the child, the easier it is to learn.

PRACTICING TOGETHER

Children can enjoy practicing their French all around your home. Encourage them to look at the furniture, toys, and objects in each room and say the French words aloud. They can use their new French vocabulary to talk to their pets and when they are playing with their friends or helping you in the kitchen. You may have some French friends who can talk to your children. All this will give your children a terrific head start when they begin formal French lessons at school.

LEARNING WITH PICTURES

Children respond very well to photographs and will enjoy finding pictures of things they know. Help them say and learn the French words for these pictures of pets, toys, and household objects around them. They can use French to count things or to tell you the colors of their clothes. They will find out the names of all the rooms in their house. Let them take you round the house and use French words to describe the things you can see.

IT'S FUN TO LEARN

Make learning fun by using the vocabulary on an everyday basis. Children need to demonstrate what they have learned by playing games. You could play "I-Spy" by choosing an object you can see and then make the sound that the word begins with or say what color it is. Ask your child to guess what French word you are thinking of and say the word aloud. The book covers important themes such as colors, counting, opposites, food, and much more. Bright and informative photographs will help the children build up their knowledge of commonly used French words and phrases in a fun way. This will give them the confidence to speak French.

HOW THE BOOK IS STRUCTURED

The key words on each page are highlighted and translated in vocabulary panels. Sentences on each page appear in both French and English to help your child understand. At the end of every section is a question-and-answer game with a puzzle for you to do together and give the child a real sense of achievement. The dictionary lists all the key words and explains how they should be pronounced. Reward certificates at the end of the book test your child's knowledge of French and develop confidence and self-esteem.

Ma maison

My home is special. Your home is special, too. Look at the pictures and say the words in French aloud. Then use your French to take your friends and family on a guided tour of your home.

La cuisine

The kitchen is a fun place to work. Everyone can help to get meals ready and then clean up.

Nous aimons préparer des gâteaux.
We like making cakes.

le rouleau à pâtisserie

le bol

les oeufs

le moule à gâteaux

Say it with me			
le tamis	le moule à gâteaux	les oeufs	le rouleau à pâtisserie
sieve	cake pan	eggs	rolling pin

Qu'il fait sale! Qui va nettoyer?
What a mess! Who will clean it up?

Anne nettoie le sol.
Anne is washing the floor.

Paul

le savon
vaisselle

Anne

l'essuie de
cuisine

le balai-éponge

Paul est en train d'essuyer.
Paul is drying the dishes.

le seau

le bol bowl	**l'essuie de cuisine** tea towel	**le savon vaisselle** dish soap	**le balai-éponge** mop	**le seau** bucket

Le salon

The living room is a family room. You can read or play games or talk, or watch television.

Je voudrais lire.
I want to read.

le chaton

le grand coussin

la balle

Mais nous, nous voulons jouer!
But we want to play!

Say it with me

les livres
books

le grand coussin
big cushion

la balle
ball

le chaton
kitten

10

Louis fait un puzzle.
Louis is doing a jigsaw puzzle.

Louis

Renata construit un château.
Renata is building a castle.

Renata

les cubes

le puzzle

De quelles couleurs sont les cubes?
What colors are the blocks?

le puzzle
jigsaw puzzle

le cube jaune
yellow block

le cube vert
green block

le cube rouge
red block

le cube bleu
blue block

11

La salle à manger

The dining room is a room where everyone can sit and talk over a meal.

Antoine est en train de mettre la table.

Antoine is setting the table.

la tasse

le couteau

la fourchette

la chaise

Antoine

la table

Say it with me

	la tasse	le couteau	la fourchette	la chaise
	mug	knife	fork	chair

J'apporte les verres.
I'll bring the glasses.

l'assiette

la pizza

deux verres

le plateau

Nous aimons manger de la pizza.
We like eating pizza.

la table
table

deux verres
two glasses

l'assiette
plate

le plateau
tray

la pizza
pizza

La salle de jeux

The play room is a special place to play in. Some children keep their toys and paints in a big toy chest.

Que peins-tu, Denis?
What are you painting, Denis?

Margot

les crayons

le dessin

Denis

la peinture

la boîte de peintures

Je peins notre maison, Margot.
I'm painting our house, Margot.

Say it with me

la peinture
painting

le dessin
drawing

la boîte de peintures
paintbox

14

Aimes-tu danser?
Do you like dancing?

les notes
de musique

le lecteur
de cassettes

J'aime écouter de la musique.
I like listening to music.

les outils

Je peux réparer les choses.
I can fix things.

les crayons
pencils

le lecteur de cassettes
cassette player

les outils
tools

les notes de musique
music notes

15

La chambre à coucher

The bedroom is the place to keep your clothes and all your favorite books and toys.

Veux-tu une histoire, Nounours?
Do you want a story, Teddy?

les livres

le nounours

Oui, s'il te plaît.
Yes, please.

Say it with me

les livres
books

le nounours
teddy bear

la bibliothèque
bookcase

la bibliothèque

le balai
mécanique

la poubelle

Ranges-tu ta chambre?
Do you clean your bedroom?

les jouets

le coussin

le balai mécanique
carpet sweeper

la poubelle
waste basket

les jouets
toys

le coussin
cushion

La salle de bain

The bathroom is full of steam and soap, and hot water. A bath gets you clean at the end of the day.

Voudrais-tu prendre un bain?
Would you like to take a bath?

le bain moussant

le savon

Non, merci.
No, thank you.

le bain

la serviette

l'éponge

Say it with me

le savon	le bain moussant	l'éponge	le bain
soap	bubble bath	sponge	bathtub

18

Je me lave les dents.
I am brushing my teeth.

Moi aussi.
Me too.

le dentifrice

la brosse à dents

le canard

le bateau

Combien de canards y a-t-il?
How many ducks are there?

le bateau boat	**la serviette** towel	**la brosse à dents** toothbrush	**le dentifrice** toothpaste	**le canard** duck

Le jardin

The garden is really hot today! Let's go out to plant flowers, play ball, and wade.

Nous sommes dans le jardin.

We are in the garden.

les fleurs

l'arrosoir

les pots de plantes

la jardinière à plantes

Combien de filles y a-t-il?

How many girls are there?

Say it with me

la jardinière à plantes	les fleurs	l'arrosoir
plant pots	flowers	watering can

Qui va attraper la balle?
Who will catch the ball?

la petite fille

le garçon

la grande fille

la piscine gonflable

L'eau est froide!
The water is cold!

la grande fille
big girl

la petite fille
little girl

le garçon
boy

la piscine gonflable
wading pool

21

Le garage

The garage is the place to keep cars and bikes, and scooters. Marie keeps her bike in the garage.

Marie a un vélo.
Marie has a bike.

Marie

le nounours

le vélo

la trottinette

Tiens-toi bien, Nounours!
Hold on, Teddy!

Say it with me

la trottinette	le nounours	le vélo	la voiture
scooter	teddy bear	bike	car

22

Nous lavons la voiture.
We are washing the car.

la roue

la voiture

le tablier

le seau

l'éponge

Est-ce que je peux aider?
Can I help?

le détergent

le détergent	l'éponge	la roue	le seau	le tablier
detergent	sponge	wheel	bucket	apron

Puzzle time

Now you know about the rooms in your home.
Write the missing words in the sentences and fill
in the crossword with the words in French.

1 Les fleurs poussent dans le jardin.

The flowers are growing in the _ _ _ _ _ _ _.

2 Les canards nagent dans le bain.

The ducks swim in the _ _ _ _ _.

3 Je laisse mon vélo dans le garage.

I put my bike in the _ _ _ _ _ _ _.

4 Je lis dans le salon.

I am reading in the _ _ _ _ _ _ _ _ _ _ _ _ _.

5 Nous prenons le dîner dans la salle à manger.

We are eating _ _ _ _ _ _ _ in the dining room.

Now try my crossword!

6 Je lave le plancher de la cuisine.

I am washing the _ _ _ _ _ _ _ floor.

25

Une journée
à la maison

A day at home gives you a chance to talk to your family and pets in French. Look at these colorful photographs of the things you do every day – and say the words aloud. You can speak French.

Se lever

Getting up in the morning is easy for some people. Other people need an alarm clock.

Bonjour, Nounours.

Good morning, Teddy.

Charlotte

le horloge

Bonjour, Charlotte.

Good morning, Charlotte.

le lit

la couverture

les chaussures

Say it with me

le lit	la couverture	le horloge	le pantalon
bed	blanket	alarm clock	pants

Voilà! Je suis habillée.

Look! I'm dressed.

la chemise

la jupe

le pantalon

la salopette

les chaussettes

J'enfile mon pull.

I am putting on my sweater.

les chaussures
shoes

la chemise
shirt

la jupe
skirt

les chaussettes
socks

la salopette
overalls

Manger le petit déjeuner

Eating breakfast is a good way to start the morning. What do you want to eat today?

Qu'y a-t-il pour le petit déjeuner?
What's for breakfast?

le pain grillé

l'oeuf sur le plat

le beurre

le petit pain

Say it with me

le beurre	le petit pain	l'oeuf sur le plat	le pain grillé
butter	bread roll	fried egg	toast

le miel

le lait

le jus de pomme

les fruits

Je mange des céréales.
I am eating cereal.

les céréales

le miel
honey

le lait
milk

le jus de pomme
apple juice

les fruits
fruit

les céréales
cereal

Jouer avec mes amis

Playing with friends is fun! They can visit you at home, and you can play lots of games.

Viens à notre petite fête.
Come to our tea party.

la théière

Peux-tu comptez les tasses?
Can you count the cups?

les nounours

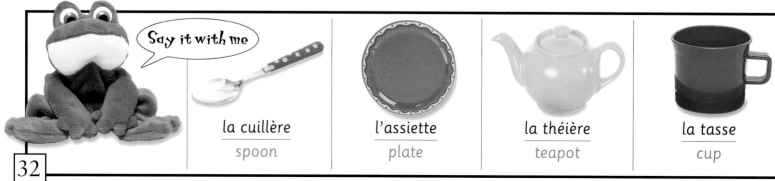

Say it with me

la cuillère	l'assiette	la théière	la tasse
spoon	plate	teapot	cup

Où est tout le monde?
Where is everyone?

Je suis dans la valise.
I am in the suitcase.

la valise

le diable dans la boîte

la fenêtre

Je suis dans la boîte.
I am in the box.

la maison

la porte

Nous sommes dans la maison.
We are in the house.

la valise	**la fenêtre**	**la maison**	**la porte**	**le diable dans la boîte**
suitcase	window	house	door	jack in the box

Une promenade au parc

A walk in the park gets you out of the house.
You can walk the dog and feed the ducks.

Allons-nous nous promener au parc?
Shall we go to the park?

Madeleine

le chien

l'écureuil

le canard

la laisse

Oui, s'il te plaît, Madeleine.
Yes, please, Madeleine.

Say it with me

| le chien | la laisse | l'écureuil |
| dog | leash | squirrel |

Nous voulons aller nourrir les canards.
We want to feed the ducks.

le sac

les bottes

Je nourris les canards.
I am feeding the ducks.

le caneton

le sac	les bottes	le canard	le caneton
bag	boots	duck	duckling

L'heure du dîner

Dinnertime is the main meal of the day.
What do you like eating best?

Qu'allons-nous manger aujourd'hui?

What shall we eat today?

les pâtes

les frites

le lait

Say it with me

les pâtes
pasta

le lait
milk

les frites
French fries

les fruits
fruit

les fruits

le poulet

le pain saucisse

le fromage

les biscuits
pour chien

les légumes

Bernard a faim.
Bernard is hungry.

le poulet	le fromage	le pain saucisse	les légumes	les biscuits pour chien
chicken	cheese	hot dog	vegetables	dog biscuits

Temps de dormir

Bedtime is sleepy time. You can read a book in bed or listen to a story, or just go to sleep.

Je n'ai pas sommeil!
I'm not sleepy!

le dragon

le lit

le chien

Combien d'animaux sont au lit?
How many animals are in bed?

Bonsoir!
Good night!

le chat

Say it with me

| le dragon | le lit | le chien |
| dragon | bed | dog |

Que portes-tu pour la nuit?
What do you wear at bedtime?

la robe
de chambre

le pyjama

Où sont mes pantoufles?
Where are my slippers?

les pantoufles

le chat	le pyjama	la robe de chambre	les pantoufles
cat	pyjamas	bathrobe	slippers

39

Missing letters?

Some words are missing from the sentences.
Can you fill them in and complete the Lost
Letters puzzle with their French names?

J'aime les céréales.

I like _ _ _ _ _ _ _ .

Le horloge donne l'heure.

The _ _ _ _ _ tells the time.

Nounours aime la maison.

_ _ _ _ _ likes the _ _ _ _ _ .

La fille mange le pain saucisse et des frites.

The ____ eats a hot dog and _____.

Le chien est brun.

The ___ is brown.

Try to find the lost letters

Dragon va au lit.

Dragon goes to ___.

céréales

h _ _ l _ _ e

n _ _ n _ _ _ _

m _ _ s _ _

_ _ l l _

f r _ _ _ _ _

_ _ _ _ n

_ _ t

L'heure de jouer

Playtime is the happiest part of the day, and you can practice your French at the same time! You can speak French while you are playing games or having fun with your friends.

Peindre

Painting is a messy thing to do! You can paint with a paintbrush or your hands or feet.

Mon pantalon a des carreaux.
My trousers have checks.

les pinceaux

la boîte
de peintures

J'aime peindre des carreaux.
I like painting checks.

Say it with me

les pinceaux	la boîte de peintures	noir	blanc
brushes	paintbox	black	white

Aimes-tu ma peinture?
Do you like my painting?

bleu

noir

jaune

blanc

rouge

vert

orange

Je peins avec mes pieds!
I'm painting with my feet!

rouge	jaune	bleu	orange	vert
red	yellow	blue	orange	green

45

Faire de la musique

Playing music is great fun. Some people play instruments, others like to dance.

l'araignée

Es-tu en train de danser?
Are you dancing?

le chaton

la danseuse

Non. J'attrape une araignée.
No. I'm catching a spider.

Say it with me

la danseuse	le chaton	l'araignée	la guitare
dancer	kitten	spider	guitar

46

Je joue de la guitare.
I play the guitar.

la flûte

le tambour

la guitare

le tambourin

le xylophone

la trompette

Peux-tu jouer du xylophone?
Can you play the xylophone?

le tambour	la flûte	le tambourin	la trompette	le xylophone
drum	recorder	tambourine	trumpet	xylophone

Se déguiser

Dressing up is an adventure. You can be a pretty fairy or a magician.

J'ai une baguette.
I have a wand.

le magicien

la baguette magique

le chapeau

la fée

Je suis un magicien.
I'm a magician.

Say it with me

la fée	la baguette magique	le chapeau	le magicien
fairy	wand	hat	magician

Vois-tu mon perroquet?
Can you see my parrot?

le cowboy

le clown

le pirate

le perroquet

Où est mon étoile?
Where's my badge?

l'étoile

Je suis un clown.
I'm a clown.

le pirate	le perroquet	le clown	le cowboy	l'étoile
pirate	parrot	clown	cowboy	badge

Faisons les courses

Playing shopping is fun. Count the food before you put it in your basket.

une baguette

Que vais-je acheter?
What shall I buy?

deux gâteaux

trois glaces

le panier

quatre bananes

Say it with me

le panier
basket

une baguette
one bread loaf

deux gâteaux
two cakes

trois glaces
three ice creams

quatre bananes
four bananas

cinq chocolats

six pommes

sept biscuits

huit cerises

neuf tomates

dix boîtes

Je fais les courses.

I am shopping.

cinq chocolats	six pommes	sept biscuits	huit cerises	neuf tomates	dix boîtes
five chocolates	*six apples*	*seven cookies*	*eight cherries*	*nine tomatoes*	*ten cans*

51

Se mouiller

Getting wet is fantastic fun.
You can splash in all the puddles.

Je suis tombé dans la flaque.
I fell in the puddle.

la pluie

les bottes

la flaque d'eau

J'aime jouer sous la pluie.
I like playing in the rain.

Say it with me

la flaque d'eau	les bottes	la pluie
puddle	boots	rain

Nous aimons pêcher sous la pluie.
We like fishing in the rain.

le chapeau

la canne à pêche

le poisson

l'imperméable

Nous avons attrapé deux poissons.
We've caught two fish!

l'imperméable
raincoat

le chapeau
hat

la canne à pêche
fishing rod

le poisson
fish

53

Jouer à des jeux

Playing games is fun. You can play with your friends and get some exercise too!

la balle

Peux-tu lancer une balle très haut?
Can you throw a ball up high?

le casque

lancer

le vélo

Qui est le gagnant de la course?
Who is winning the race?

Say it with me

la balle ball	lancer throw	le casque helmet	le vélo bike

54

Nous aimons faire du sport.
We like sport.

les patins à roulettes

la planche à roulettes

le football

Qui est en haut?
Who is high?

les quilles

sauter

Qui est en bas?
Who is low?

le football	les patins à roulettes	la planche à roulettes	les quilles	sauter
soccer ball	roller skates	skateboard	bowling pins	jump

Puzzle time

Can you count from one to six? Here are some clues. The French numbers are in the Word Square.

Un garçon lance une balle.
___ boy throwing a ball.

Deux garçons pêchent.
___ boys fishing.

Trois instruments de musique.
_____ musical instruments.

Quatre enfants sautent.
_ _ _ _ children jumping.

Le clown jongle avec cinq balles.
The clown is juggling _ _ _ _ balls.

Find the French numbers in my word square

Six empreintes de pieds.
_ _ _ footprints.

a	q	u	a	t	r	e
t	h	a	b	r	l	o
r	o	t	c	o	a	q
g	u	r	c	i	n	q
o	n	i	a	s	m	u
d	e	u	x	a	n	o
c	h	i	e	s	i	x

How French works

Encourage your child to enjoy learning French and go further in the language. You may find these basic tips on how the French language works helpful. Consult the dictionary, since it lists all the key words in the book and will help you and your child pronounce the words correctly.

MASCULINE/FEMININE

All nouns in French are either masculine (le, un) or feminine (la, une). "Les" or "des" are for plural words whether they are feminine or masculine.

COMPARING THINGS

When we want to compare things in English, we say they are, for example, small, smaller or smallest. This is the pattern in French.

FRENCH	ENGLISH
Il est petit	He is small
Il est plus petit que moi	He is smaller than me
Il est le plus petit	He is the smallest

ADJECTIVES

As a general rule, an "e" is added to the end of the adjective if the noun is feminine (e.g. "la table verte"). Do not add an "e" if the noun is masculine (e.g. "le serpent vert").

PERSONAL PRONOUNS

Remember that "il" is masculine and "elle" is feminine. The plurals are "ils" and "elles".

FRENCH	ENGLISH
je	I
tu	you (singular)
il *or* elle	he or she
nous	we
vous	you (plural)
ils *or* elles	they

"Tu" is used for talking to people you know or to animals. "Vous" is used when talking to someone you don't know and are being polite. It is also used when you are talking to more than one person.

VERBS

French verbs change their endings depending on which personal pronoun and tense are used. This book uses only the present tense but there are other tenses in French including the past and the future.

Help your child find the language pattern that emerges in the endings of the verbs. Point out that in the verbs here, "tu" always ends "-es" and "vous" always ends "-ez". Explain that the extra "e" in "Nous mangeons" is to soften the "g" and make it easier to say the words. Play a game by saying the first word aloud – "Je", "Tu". Let your child answer – "marche", "marches".

Here are four simple verbs in the present tense. Look at the ends of the words and say the French out loud.

FRENCH	ENGLISH
marcher	**to walk**
Je marche	I walk
Tu marches	You walk
Il/elle marche	He/she walks
Nous marchons	We walk
Vous marchez	You walk
Ils/elles marchent	They walk

FRENCH	ENGLISH
sauter	**to jump**
Je saute	I jump
Tu sautes	You jump
Il/elle saute	He/she jumps
Nous sautons	We jump
Vous sautez	You jump
Ils/elles sautent	They jump

FRENCH	ENGLISH
aimer	**to like**
J'aime	I like
Tu aimes	You like
Il/elle aime	He/she likes
Nous aimons	We like
Vous aimez	You like
Ils/elles aiment	They like

FRENCH	ENGLISH
manger	**to eat**
Je mange	I eat
Tu manges	You eat
Il/elle mange	He/she eats
Nous mangeons	We eat
Vous mangez	You eat
Ils/elles mangent	They eat

Pronunciation Key

FRENCH	SAY	EXAMPLE
a, à	ah	chat: sha
an, en	on	blanc: blon
e, eu	uh	renard: ruh-nar
é	ay	réveil: ray-vehy
ê, è, ai	eh	tête: teht
eau, o	oh	bateau: ba-toh
eil, eille	ehy	abeille: a-behy
euil, euille	euhy	feuilles: feuhy
g, ge, j	jsh	rouge: roojsh
gn	ny	oignons: o-nyon
i	ee	lit: lee
in	ah	lapin: la-pah
lle	y	fille: feey
oi	wa	poisson: pwa-sson
on	on	chaton: sha-ton
ou	oo	nounours: noo-noors
ouille	ooy	grenouille: gruh-nooy
u	ew	musique: mew-zeek
ui	wee	cuillère: kwee-yehr`
un	uhn	brun: bruhn

Le dictionnaire

ENGLISH	FRENCH	SAY
A		
alarm clock	le horloge	*luh hor-low-jsh*
apple	la pomme	*la pomm*
apple juice	le jus de pomme	*luh jew duh pomm*
apron	le tablier	*luh tab-lee-ay*
B		
badge	l'étoile	*lay-twal*
bag	le sac	*luh sak*
ball	la balle	*la bal*
banana	la banane	*la ba-nan*
basket	le panier	*luh pa-nee-ay*
bath	le bain	*luh bah*
bathrobe	la robe de chambre	*la rob duh shon-br*
bathroom	la salle de bain	*la sall duh bah*
bed	le lit	*luh lee*
bedroom	la chambre à coucher	*la shom-br ah coo-shay*
bike	le vélo	*luh vaylo*
block	le cube	*luh kewb*
boat	le bateau	*luh ba-toh*
bookcase	la bibliothèque	*la bee-bleeo-tehk*
books	les livres	*leh lee-vruh*
boots	les bottes	*leh bot*

Colors

ENGLISH	FRENCH	SAY
black	noir	*nwar*
blue	bleu	*bluh*
green	vert	*vehr*
grey	gris	*gree*
orange	orange	*o-ronjsh*
pink	rose	*rohz*
red	rouge	*roojsh*
white	blanc	*blon*
yellow	jaune	*jshonn*

ENGLISH	FRENCH	SAY
bowl	le bol	*luh bol*
bowling pins	les quilles	*leh keey*
boy	le garçon	*luh gar-sson*
bread loaf	la baguette	*la ba-geht*
bread roll	le petit pain	*luh puh-tee pah*
breakfast	le petit déjeuner	*luh puh-tee dayj-nay*
brushes	les pinceaux	*leh pah-sso*
bubble bath	le bain moussant	*luh bah moo-sson*
bucket	le seau	*luh sso*
butter	le beurre	*luh buhr*
C		
cake	le gâteau	*luh ga-toh*
cake pan	le moule à gâteau	*luh mool a ga-toh*
can	la boîte	*la bwat*
car	la voiture	*la vwa-toor*
carpet sweeper	le balai mécanique	*luh ba-leh may-ka-neek*
cassette player	le lecteur de cassettes	*luh lek-tuhr duh cass-ett*
cat	le chat	*luh sha*
cereal	les céréales	*leh see-re-ahl*
chair	la chaise	*la shehz*
cheese	le fromage	*luh fro-majsh*
cherries	les cerises	*leh suh-reez*
chicken	le poulet	*leh poo-leh*
chocolates	les chocolats	*leh shok-oh-lah*
clown	le clown	*luh kloon*
cookies	les biscuits	*leh beess-kwee*
cowboy	le cowboy	*luh kowboy*
cup	la tasse	*la tass*
cushion	le coussin	*luh koo-ssah*
D		
dancer	la danseuse	*la don-ssuhs*
detergent	le détergent	*luh day-tehr-jshon*
dining room	la salle à manger	*la sall ah mon-jay*
dinner	le dîner	*leh dee-nay*
dish soap	le savon vaisselle	*luh ssa-von veh-ssehl*
dog	le chien	*luh shee-ah*
dog biscuits	les biscuits pour chien	*leh bees-kwee poor shee-ah*

Days of the week

ENGLISH	FRENCH	SAY
Monday	lundi	*luhn-dee*
Tuesday	mardi	*mar-dee*
Wednesday	mercredi	*mehr-kruh-dee*
Thursday	jeudi	*jshuh-dee*
Friday	vendredi	*von-druh-dee*
Saturday	samedi	*samuh-dee*
Sunday	dimanche	*dee-monsh*

ENGLISH	FRENCH	SAY
door	la porte	*la port*
dragon	le dragon	*luh dra-gong*
drawing	le dessin	*luh deh-ssah*
drum	le tambour	*luh ton-boor*
duck	le canard	*luh ka-nar*
duckling	le caneton	*luh ka-nuh-ton*

E and F

eggs	les oeufs	*leh zuh*
fairy	la fée	*la fay*
fish	le poisson	*luh pwa-sson*
fishing rod	la canne à pêche	*la kan a pehsh*
flower pot	le pot de fleurs	*luh po duh fluhr*
flowers	les fleurs	*leh fluhr*
fork	la fourchette	*la foor-sheht*
French fries	les frites	*leh freet*
fried egg	l'oeuf sur le plat	*luhf sewr luh pla*
fruit	les fruits	*leh fwee*

G and H

garage	le garage	*luh gar-arj*
garden	le jardin	*luh jar-dan*
girl	la fille	*la feey*
glass	le verre	*luh vehr*
guitar	la guitare	*la gee-tar*
hat	le chapeau	*luh sha-poh*
helmet	la casque	*la kask*
honey	le miel	*luh mee-ehl*

ENGLISH	FRENCH	SAY
hot dog	le pain saucisse	*luh pahn so-sseess*
house	la maison	*la meh-zon*

I and J

ice cream	la glace	*la glass*
jack in the box	le diable dans la boîte	*luh dee-abl don la bwat*
jigsaw	le puzzle	*luh pewzl*

K

kitchen	la cuisine	*la kwee-zeen*
kitten	le chaton	*luh sha-ton*
knife	le couteau	*luh koo-toh*

L and M

leash	la laisse	*la lehss*
living room	le salon	*luh sah-lon*
magician	le magicien	*luh ma-jee-ssee-ah*
mechanical	mécanique	*may-ka-neek*
milk	le lait	*luh leh*
mop	le balai-éponge	*luh ba-leh ay ponjsh*
mug	la tasse	*la tass*
music notes	les notes de musique	*leh not duh mew-zeek*

Months of the year

ENGLISH	FRENCH	SAY
January	janvier	*jshon-vee-ay*
February	février	*fay-vree-ay*
March	mars	*marss*
April	avril	*av-reel*
May	mai	*meh*
June	juin	*jshew-ah*
July	juillet	*jshwee-eh*
August	août	*oot*
September	septembre	*sehp-tom-br*
October	octobre	*ok-tobr*
November	novembre	*no-vom-br*
December	décembre	*day-som-br*

ENGLISH	FRENCH	SAY

O and P

ENGLISH	FRENCH	SAY
overalls	la salopette	*la sa-lo-peht*
paintbox	la boîte de peintures	*la bwat duh pah-tewr*
painting	la peinture	*la pahn-tewr*
pajamas	le pyjama	*luh pee-ja-ma*
pants	le pantalon	*luh pon-ta-lon*
parrot	le perroquet	*luh pehro-keh*
pasta	les pâtes	*leh paat*
pencils	les crayons	*leh kreh-yon*
pirate	le pirate	*luh pee-rat*
pizza	la pizza	*la pee-za*
plant pot	le pot de plantes	*luh po duh plahnt*
plate	l'assiette	*la-ssee-eht*
play room	la salle de jeux	*la sall duh juh*
puddle	la flaque d'eau	*la flak doh*

R

ENGLISH	FRENCH	SAY
rain	la pluie	*la plwee*
raincoat	l'imperméable	*lahm-pehr-may-ahbl*
recorder	la flûte	*la flewt*
roller skates	les patins à roulettes	*leh pa-tah a roo-leht*

S

ENGLISH	FRENCH	SAY
scooter	la trottinette	*la tro-tee-neht*
shirt	la chemise	*la shuh-meez*
shoes	les chaussures	*leh sho-ssewr*

Numbers

ENGLISH	FRENCH	SAY
one	un	*uhn*
two	deux	*duh*
three	trois	*trwa*
four	quatre	*katr*
five	cinq	*sahnk*
six	six	*seess*
seven	sept	*seht*
eight	huit	*weet*
nine	neuf	*nuhf*
ten	dix	*deess*

ENGLISH	FRENCH	SAY
sieve	le tamis	*luh ta-mee*
skateboard	la planche à roulettes	*la plonsh a roo-leht*
skirt	la jupe	*la jewp*
slippers	les pantoufles	*leh pon-toofl*
soap	le savon	*luh sa-von*
soccer ball	le football	*luh football*
socks	les chaussettes	*leh sho-sseht*
soft toy	la peluche	*la puh-lewsh*
spider	l'araignée	*la-reh-nyay*
sponge	l'éponge	*lay-ponjsh*
spoon	la cuillère	*la kwee-yehr*
squirrel	l'écureuil	*lay-kew-reuhy*
suitcase	la valise	*la va-leez*
sun	le soleil	*luh so-lehy*

T

ENGLISH	FRENCH	SAY
table	la table	*la tabl*
tambourine	le tambourin	*luh ton-boo-rah*
teapot	la théière	*la tay-ee-ehr*
tea towel	l'essuie de cuisine	*leh-sswee duh kwee-zeen*
teddy bear	le nounours	*luh noo-noorss*
to jump	sauter	*so-tay*
to throw	lancer	*lon-say*
toast	le pain grillé	*luh pahn gree-yay*
tomato	la tomate	*la toe-maat*
tools	les outils	*leh zoo-teel*
toothbrush	la brosse à dents	*la bross a don*
toothpaste	le dentifrice	*luh don-tee-frees*
towel	la serviette	*la sehr-vee-et*
toys	les jouets	*leh jshoo-eh*
tray	le plateau	*luh pla-toh*
trumpet	la trompette	*la tromm-pet*

V, W and X

ENGLISH	FRENCH	SAY
vegetables	les légumes	*leh lay-gewm*
wading pool	la piscine gonflable	*la pee-sseen gon-fla-bl*
wand	la baguette magique	*la ba-geht ma-jeek*
waste basket	la poubelle	*la poo-behl*
watering can	l'arrosoir	*la-roh-zwar*
wheel	la roue	*la roo-uh*
window	la fenêtre	*la fuh-nehtr*
xylophone	le xylophone	*luh zee-lo-fon*

This is to certify that

_____

can count
from one to ten
in French

Date _____

This is to certify that

_____

can name
six colors
in French

Date _____

This is to certify that

_____

can name
five toys
in French

Date _____

This is to certify that

_____

can name the
rooms in a house
in French

Date _____

This edition is published by Lorenz Books

Lorenz Books is an imprint of Anness Publishing Ltd
Hermes House, 88–89 Blackfriars Road, London SE1 8HA
tel. 020 7401 2077; fax 020 7633 9499
www.lorenzbooks.com
info@anness.com

© Anness Publishing Ltd 2002

Published in the USA by Lorenz Books, Anness Publishing Inc.
27 West 20th Street, New York, NY 10011
fax 212 807 6813

Published in Australia by Pan Macmillan Australia
Level 18, St Martins Tower, 31 Market St, Sydney, NSW 2000
tel. 1300 135 113; fax 1300 135 103; email customer.service@macmillan.com.au

This edition distributed in the UK by Aurum Press Ltd
25 Bedford Avenue, London WC1B 3AT
tel. 020 7637 3225; fax 020 7580 2469

This edition distributed in the USA by National Book Network
4720 Boston Way, Lanham, MD 20706
tel. 301 459 3366; fax 301 459 1705
www.nbnbooks.com

This edition distributed in Canada by General Publishing
895 Don Mills Road, 400–402 Park Centre, Toronto, Ontario M3C 1W3
tel. 416 445 3333; fax 416 445 5991
www.genpub.com

This edition distributed in New Zealand by David Bateman Ltd
30 Tarndale Grove, Off Bush Road, Albany, Auckland
tel. (09) 415 7664; fax (09) 415 8892

Publisher: Joanna Lorenz
Managing Editor: Linda Fraser
Editor: Joy Wotton
Designer: Maggi Howells
Jacket Designer: Roger McWilliam
Photography: Jane Burton, John Daniels, John Freeman,
Robert Pickett, Kim Taylor, Lucy Tizard

The publishers wish to thank all the children
who appear in this book.

10 9 8 7 6 5 4 3 2 1

Et maintenant, tu peux parler français!